BLAZERS

SUPER SPEED

INDY CAR
Racing

BY LORI POLYDOROS

Reading Consultant:
Barbara J. Fox
Reading Specialist
Professor Emerita
North Carolina State University

Content Consultant:
Donald Davidson
Historian, Indianapolis Motor Speedway
Indianapolis, Indiana

CAP
a

Blazers Books are published by Capstone Press,
1710 Roe Crest Drive, North Mankato, Minnesota 56003
www.capstonepub.com

Library of Congress Cataloging-in-Publication Data
Polydoros, Lori.
 Indy car racing / by Lori Polydoros.
   p. cm. — (Blazers. Super speed.)
 Includes bibliographical references and index.
 Summary: "Describes Indy cars and Indy car racing, including safety features and rules governing
Indy car races"—Provided by publisher.
  ISBN 978-1-4296-9995-2 (library binding)
  ISBN 978-1-4765-1362-1 (eBook PDF)
 1. Indianapolis Speedway Race—History—Juvenile literature. 2. Automobile racing—Juvenile
literature. I. Title.
  GV1033.5.I55P65 2013
  796.7209772'52—dc23   2012028359

Editorial Credits
Mari Bolte, editor; Kyle Grenz, designer; Eric Manske, production specialist

Photo Credits
AP Images, 26; Dreamstime: Carroteater, 24 (top), 27, Dwebrown, 7 (bottom), 20–21, Splan06, 24
(bottom); Getty Images: Donald Miralle, 11 (top), Jonathan Ferrey, 7 (top), Robert Laberge, 22–23;
Newscom: AFP/Getty Images/Nelson Almeida, 16–17, AiWire "Ai Wire Photo Service"/Russell
LaBounty, cover, Cal Sport Media/Tom Turrill, 14, Kyodo, 29, MCT/Kim Hairston, 19, ZUMA Press/
Ron Bijlsma, 5, 8–9, 12–13; Wikimedia/Sarah Stierch, 11 (bottom)

Artistic Effects
Shutterstock: 1xpert, My Portfolio, rodho

Printed in the United States of America in Brainerd, Minnesota.
092012   006938BANGS13

TABLE OF CONTENTS

SKILL AND DARING

A group of Indy cars zips around a sharp turn at top speed. Reaching speeds greater than 200 miles (322 kilometers) per hour, the cars race for the finish line. Drivers use skill, bravery, and the latest **technology** to race safely.

technology—the use of science to do practical things, such as designing complex machines

BUILT FOR SPEED AND SAFETY

Indy cars are wide and flat. They have wings and **side pods**. These features help keep the car balanced at high speeds and around turns. Each car also has a **safety cell**.

side pod—a curved panel along each side of an Indy car that keeps the car balanced

safety cell—a protected cockpit area in which the driver sits

SAFETY CELL

SIDE POD

Indy cars are called open-wheel racers. On these cars, the tires are not covered. The open-wheel design puts drivers at higher risk for accidents. Wheel-to-wheel contact at high speeds can cause cars to fly up in the air.

FAST FACT

Formula One cars are also open-wheel racers. These cars race on tracks that have many curves and turns.

Indy car engines run on **ethanol** instead of gasoline. This special fuel increases the car's speed. The high speeds make the tires as hot as boiling water. The tarlike grip helps the car stick to the track.

ethanol—a biofuel made from crops such as corn and sugarcane

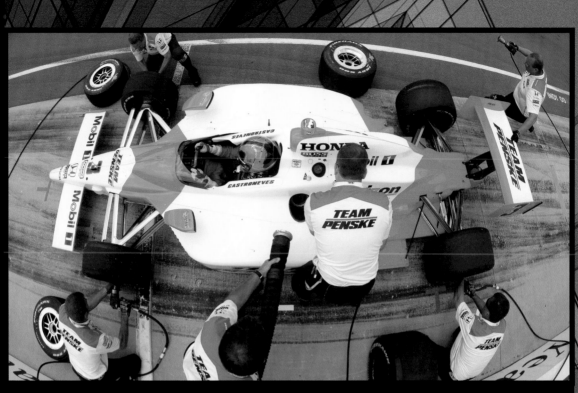

A pit crew can refuel a car and change its tires in 10 seconds.

RACING SLICKS

PHOTO DIAGRAM

1. **REAR WING**

2. **AIR BOX**

3. **ROLL HOOP**

4. **HEAD PROTECTION**

5. **COCKPIT**

6. **CARBON FIBER FRAME**

7. **FRONT WING**

8. **RACING SLICKS**

9. **SIDE POD**

10. **FUEL TANK (ETHANOL)**

11. **ENGINE**

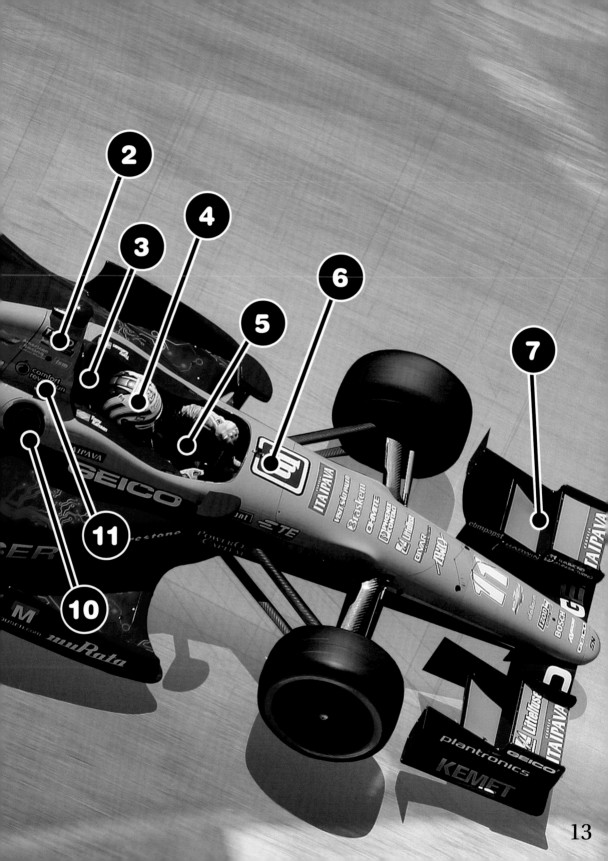

FAST FACT

Indy car drivers must wear protective shoes, socks, gloves, underwear, and head socks.

Indy cars can go from 0 to 100 miles (161 km) per hour in less than three seconds. Safety is always a concern while racing at such high speeds. All drivers must wear helmets and **fire suits**.

fire suit—a protective body suit that helps resist fire; fire suits are made with a nylonlike material called Nomex

Even with the latest safety features, accidents still happen. Since 2000 there have been three deadly accidents. In 2011 champion Dan Wheldon lost his life after a crash.

a crash at the Anhembi racetrack in São Paulo, Brazil, in 2011

RACING RULES

Indy cars race on oval tracks called speedways. They also race on **street courses**. These courses have narrow, quick corners. The turns make it very difficult for cars to drive side-by-side.

street course—an Indy car race held on city streets that have been blocked off

The Baltimore Grand Prix is raced on a street course.

To **qualify** for races, drivers compete for start position. Except for the Indianapolis 500, racers get one try. The fastest car in the qualifying round gets the **pole position**. The other cars line up from fastest to slowest.

qualify—to earn a starting spot in a race by completing timed laps

pole position—the inside spot in the front row at the beginning of a race

The oldest and most famous Indy car race is the Indianapolis 500. The race is 200 laps, or 500 miles (805 km) long. Drivers must qualify for the race over a two-day period.

FAST FACT

Drivers get three chances to qualify for the Indianapolis 500.

An Indy 500 qualifying run is four laps, or 10 miles (16 km) long. Each car runs alone against a timer. Slower cars are "bumped" from the starting field by faster cars. The fastest 33 drivers go on to race in the Indianapolis 500.

FAST FACT

The first day of qualifying rounds at Indianapolis is called pole day. The second day is called bump day.

The first Indy 500 race was finished in six hours, 42 minutes. In 2012 the race took just over three hours.

Fans flocked to the first Indianapolis 500 in 1911. Ever since, the stands have been crowded with people eager to watch the event. More than 250,000 fans attend the famous race each year.

FAST FACT

The Indy 500 was first shown on TV in 1949. It was the first TV program seen in the city of Indianapolis.

INDY FANS AROUND THE WORLD

Indy car races are watched around the globe. Every year millions of fans in more than 210 countries watch their favorite Indy cars. Drivers such as Helio Castroneves, Dario Franchitti, and Scott Dixon show off the best of Indy car racing.

SCOTT DIXON

GLOSSARY

ethanol (ETH-uh-nal)—a biofuel made from crops such as corn and sugarcane

fire suit (FYR SOOT)—a protective body suit that helps resist fire; fire suits are made with a nylonlike material called Nomex

pole position (POHL puh-ZISH-uhn)—the inside spot in the front row at the beginning of a race

qualify (KWAHL-uh-fye)—to earn a starting spot in a race by completing timed laps

safety cell (SAYF-tee SEL)—a protected cockpit area in which the driver sits; the safety cell includes the cockpit, the bottom of the car, and the car frame

side pods (SIDE PODS)—a curved panel along each side of an Indy car that keeps the car balanced

street course (STREET KORSS)—an Indy car race held on city streets that have been blocked off

technology (tek-NOL-uh-jee)—the use of science to do practical things, such as designing complex machines

READ MORE

Georgiou, Tyrone. *Indy Cars.* Fast Lane. New York: Gareth Stevens Pub., 2012.

Maurer, Tracy Nelson. *Stock Car Racing.* Super Speed. North Mankato, Minn.: Capstone Pub., 2013.

Sheen, Barbara. *Janet Guthrie: Indy Car Racing Pioneer.* Innovators. Detroit: Kidhaven Press, 2010.

INTERNET SITES

FactHound offers a safe, fun way to find Internet sites related to this book. All of the sites on FactHound have been researched by our staff.

Here's all you do:

Visit *www.facthound.com*

Type in this code: 9781429699952

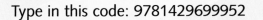

INDEX